NATURE WATCH

BEARS
and
PANDAS

MICHAEL BRIGHT

Consultant: Dr. Douglas Richardson,
Zoological Director, Rome Zoo

C O N

Published by Anness Publishing Ltd,
Blaby Road, Wigston, Leicestershire LE18 4SE
Email: info@anness.com
Web: www.annesspublishing.com

Anness Publishing has a new picture agency outlet for
images for publishing, promotions or advertising. Please
visit our website www.practicalpictures.com for more
information.

Publisher: Joanna Lorenz
Managing Editor, Children's Books: Gilly Cameron Cooper
Senior Editor: Nicole Pearson
Editor: Charlotte Hurdman
Designer: Caroline Reeves
Picture Researcher: Cathy Stastny
Photographer: John Freeman
Illustrators: David Webb, Vanessa Card, Julian Baker
Production Controller: Ann Childers
Editorial Reader: Diane Ashmore

Special thanks to Nick Lindsay, Curator of the
Whipsnade Wildlife Park, for his help on this book.

ETHICAL TRADING POLICY
Because of our ongoing ecological investment programme,
you, as our customer, can have the pleasure and
reassurance of knowing that a tree is being cultivated on
your behalf to naturally replace the materials used to
make the book you are holding. For further information
about this scheme, go to www.annesspublishing.com/trees

© Anness Publishing Ltd.2000, 2011

PICTURE CREDITS
b = bottom, t = top, c = centre, l = left, r = right
ADRIAN LISTER: 48tr. B & C ALEXANDER: 55tr, 58tl, 44br,
45bl, 57b; Bob Wilson: 41bl. BBC NATURAL HISTORY UNIT:
Doug Allan: 56tl; Gerry Ellis: 25bl; Jeff Foott: 27tl, 55br, 59tl;
Martha Holmes: 28tl; Hans Christoph Kappel: 27br; Tom Lazar:
25tr; Mary Ann McDonald: 52bl; Thomas D. Mangelsen: 19tr, 56b;
Klaus Nigge: 13bl; Pete Oxford: 60tr; Lynn M. Stone: 11cr; David
Welling: 57br. BRIDGEMAN ART LIBRARY: Oxford University
Museum of Natural History: 11b. BRITISH MUSEUM: 14bl.
BRUCE COLEMAN: Erwin & Peggy Bauer: 4bl, 20br, 47tl, 58tl;
Thomas Buchholz: 60bl; Sophy & Michael Day: 57tr, 54tr; Stephen
Kraseman: 45br; Joe McDonald: 52tr; Hans Reinhard: 8br, 9tr, 55cl;
Leonard Lee Rue: 36tr; John Shaw: 7br, 9br, 50bl; Joseph Van
Wormer: 47cr. E T ARCHIVE: 20tr; Archaeological Museum, Sofia:
61tl. FLPA: Rolf Bender: 35bl; P. Davey: 55tr; Gerard Lacey: 12bl,
46tl; Mark Newman: 6br, 12tr, 15bl, 15tl, 24bl, 25br, 34tr, 40tr, 40b,
51br, 55tr; Fritz Polking: 8tl, 51tl; Cordier/Sunset: 19tl; T.
Leeson/Sunset: 47bl. HEATHER ANGEL: 5c, 17tl, 25tl, 25tr, 34bl,
42tr, 54bl, 55cl. IMAGE BANK: Paul McCormick: 61tr; Joseph Van
Os: 10tr, 18bl. L B & W: 4tr. MARY EVANS: 12br, 16tr, 58bl; J M
Gleeson in The Outing Magazine 1906, vol 49, p289: 55tl;
Whittaker's Star Atlas, Plate 6: 44tr. NHPA: B & C Alexander: 29bl,
29cr; Daniel Heuclin: 58bl; T. Kitchin & V. Hurst: 6c, 59bl; Stephen
Kraseman: 29tl, 55br, 57cl, 59tl; Rob Planck: 59br; B. Hanumantha
Rao: 45br; Andy Rouse: 35cr, 51tr, 55br; Kevin Schafer: 26bl; John
Shaw: 35bl, 52tr. OXFORD SCIENTIFIC FILMS: Michael
Austerman: 7bl; Liz Bomford: 11cl; John Brown: 42bl; John
Chellman: 50tl; Judd Cooney: 24br; Daniel J. Cox: 5bl, 15tr, 17br,
17cl, 18tr, 21bl, 24tr, 25bl, 50tr, 34br, 55t, 37tl, 46br, 50br; Richard
Foster: 55tl; David C. Fritts: 15br, 26tr, 27bl; Dan Guravich: 16bl,
44bl; Djuro Huber: 51bl; Frank Huber: 42br; Keith & Liz Laidler:
22tl; Zig Leszczynski: 6tl, 15br; Stephen Mills: 51tl; Ben Osborne:
59tr; Stan Osolinski: 41tl; Stouffer Productions: 50bl; Norbert
Rosing: 51tr, 57cl, 41c, 61br; David Shale: 58br; Vivek Sinha: 21br;
Keren Su: 14tr, 22br; Konrad Wothe: 57cr. PAPILIO: 51bl.
PLANET EARTH: Jim Brandenburg: 17tr; Brian Kenny: 4br; Ken
Lucas: 11tr, 14br; Louise Murray: 5tl; Nikita Ovsyanikov: 21tr, 51br;
Tom Walker: 7tl, 19br, 21tl, 26tr. ROGER TIDMAN: 52b, 59bl, 59c.
TONY STONE IMAGES: Tim Davis: 25tl; David Hiser: 56br.
WWF FOR NATURE 1986: 55tl.

T E N T S

The Bear Facts

Bears may look large, cuddly and appealing, but in reality they are enormously powerful animals. Bears are mammals with bodies covered in thick fur. They are heavily built with short tails and large claws. All bears are carnivores (meat-eaters), but most enjoy a very mixed diet with the occasional snack of meat. The exception is the polar bear, which feasts on the blubber (fat) of seals. There are eight living species of bear: the brown bear, American black bear, Asiatic black bear, polar bear, sun bear, sloth bear, spectacled bear and the giant panda. They live in both cold and tropical regions of the world. Bears are loners and their nature is unpredictable, which makes them potentially dangerous to people.

WINNIE-THE-POOH
The lovable teddy bear Winnie-the-Pooh was created by A.A. Milne. Like real bears he loved honey. Teddy bears became popular as toys in the early 1900s. The President of the U.S.A. Theodore Roosevelt refused to shoot a bear cub on a hunting trip. Toy bears went on sale soon after known as "teddy's bears".

◀ **BEAR FACE**
The brown bear shares the huge dog-like head and face of all bears. Bears have prominent noses, but relatively small eyes and ears. This is because they mostly rely on their sense of smell to help them find food.

▲ **BIG FLAT FEET**
A polar bear's feet are broad, flat and furry. The five long, curved claws cannot be retracted (pulled back). One swipe could kill a seal instantly.

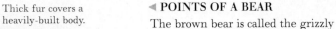

Thick fur covers a
heavily-built body.

◄ POINTS OF A BEAR

The brown bear is called the grizzly
bear in North America. Fully-grown
brown bears weigh nearly half a tonne.
They fear no other animals apart from
humans. They can chase prey at high
speed, but they rarely bother as
they feed mainly on plants.

A bear has a large head,
with small eyes and
erect, rounded ears.

The long, prominent,
dog-like snout
dominates the face.

A bear's main
strength is in its
massive shoulders
and front legs.

Its broad, flat feet
have long claws.

▲ GIANT PANDA

China's giant panda, with its distinctive
black and white coat, is a very unusual
bear. Unlike most other bears, which
will eat anything, pandas feed almost
exclusively on the bamboo plant.

◄ ARCTIC NOMAD

Most bears lead a solitary life. The polar bear
wanders alone across the Arctic sea ice.
Usually it will not tolerate other
bears. The exceptions are
bears that congregate at
rubbish dumps, or
mothers accompanied
by their cubs as
shown here.

5

Sloth bear
(Melursus ursinus)

Size of a Bear

The two largest bears in the world are the powerful polar bear and the brown bears of Kodiak Island, Alaska. Kodiak bears grow up to 2.8m long and weigh, on average, up to 443kg, while polar bears have a maximum length of 3m and weigh as much as 650kg. Brown bears in Europe and Asia are generally smaller than grizzlies (American brown bears). The largest is the Kamchatka brown bear of eastern Russia. A full size adult grizzly weighs as much as a bison and even the smallest is bigger than a wolf. The smallest bear is the sun bear at 1.4m long and weighing 65kg. In between are American and Asiatic black bears (both 1.7m long and up to 120kg), the spectacled bear (2.1m long, up to 200kg) and the sloth bear (1.9m long, up to 115kg).

▲ **SLOTH BEAR**
Long curved claws, a mobile snout and long fur are the distinguishing features of the sloth bear. It lives in India and Sri Lanka and feeds mainly on insects called termites and fruit.

American black bear
(Ursus americanus)

▼ **SPECTACLED BEAR**
The South American spectacled bear gets its name from the distinctive markings on its face. It is the only bear found in South America and is a good climber.

Spectacled bear
(Tremarctos ornatus)

▲ **AMERICAN BLACK BEAR**
There are ten times as many black bears as brown bears living in the forests of North America. Black bears resemble small brown bears except that they lack a shoulder hump.

Polar bear
(Ursus maritimus)

◀ ICE GIANT

The male polar bear is a giant among
bears. It is bigger than most brown bears,
but less robustly built, with a longer
head and neck. Female polar bears are
much smaller, weighing less than half
a fully-grown adult male. Polar bears
live in the frozen wastes of the Arctic.
They can swim in the icy sea, protected
by insulating fur and layers of thick fat.

Brown bear
(Ursus arctos)

▶ BIG BROWN BEARS

The brown bear is the most widely found bear,
living in Europe, Asia and North America. Its size
varies in different parts of the world. This is due
to diet and climate rather than any genetic
differences. For example, large Kodiak bears
catch a lot of protein-rich salmon.

Did you know? The heaviest known Kodiak brown bears weigh up to 750kg.

▼ THE SUN BEAR

The sun bear is the smallest of all the bears.
It lives in the thick forests of South-east
Asia. Because it lives in a hot tropical
climate, the sun bear also has
a short coat. Its feet have naked soles
and long, curved claws, which can grip
well when climbing trees.

Sun bear
(Helarctos malayanus)

Giant panda
(Ailuropoda melanoleuca)

Giant Pandas

Scientists have argued for many years about whether or not the giant panda is a bear. In 1869, the first Western naturalist to see a giant panda identified it as a bear. But a year later, scientists examined a panda skeleton and decided it was more like a raccoon. This was because the giant panda's skeleton shared some features with the red panda, an earlier discovery that had been grouped with the raccoon family. The giant panda certainly looks like a bear, but it does not behave like one. It does not hibernate, although it lives in places with very cold winters. It rarely roars like a bear, but tends to bleat. Recent genetic studies and comparisons with other animals, however, indicate that the panda's nearest relatives are bears and that the giant panda is indeed a bear.

▲ UP A TREE

Giant pandas sometimes climb trees to avoid enemies. They also scrape trees with their claws. This is a sign that says KEEP OUT to other pandas. Pandas are about 1.7m long and weigh up to 125kg. They are the only surviving members of the earliest group of bears to evolve. Fossils of giant pandas have only ever been discovered in Thailand and China.

▶ RED PANDA

The red panda is a member of the raccoon family and lives in the high bamboo forests of southern Asia. It has several similarities to the giant panda, including skull shape, tooth structure and a false thumb to hold bamboo.

Red panda
(Ailurus fulgens)

▶ BAMBOO BEAR

The giant panda of western China spends 10 to 12 hours a day eating bamboo. Its massive head contains large chewing muscles needed to break up the tough bamboo. It has a simple stomach and short gut, however, which are features of a meat-eating carnivore and make digesting bamboo hard work. The giant panda's large shoulders and reduced hindquarters give it a curious, shambling walk.

Giant panda
(*Ailuropoda melanoleuca*)

Raccoon (*Procyon lotor*)

▲ FALSE THUMB

The giant panda has a false thumb on its forepaw. This is a modified wrist bone used to hold narrow bamboo shoots. A giant panda's massive skull is quite distinct from the smaller, more slender skull of the raccoon. The raccoon (*Procyon lotor*) does not have a false thumb, unlike its relative the red panda.

▼ AMERICAN BANDIT

The inquisitive raccoon is a close relative of bears. It lives in North America and uses its front paws to capture small aquatic prey, such as freshwater crayfish. It also scavenges through the remains of human waste.

Raccoon
(*Procyon lotor*)

Bones and Teeth

Bears have a large and massive skull, a solidly built skeleton, relatively short and stocky limbs, a small tail and short feet. Each foot has five equal-sized digits (toes), with strong, curved claws for digging and tearing.
The claws cannot be retracted (pulled back) so are constantly worn down. In most bears' jaws, the carnassial teeth (large meat-shearing teeth) common to all carnivores are reduced or even missing. Instead, bears have broad flat molars for crushing plant food. Only the polar bear has flesh-slicing carnassials to deal with its animal prey. The sloth bear is also unusual because it lacks the inner pair of upper incisors (front teeth). This helps it suck up insects from their nests.

▲ **A MIGHTY ROAR**
As this bear roars, it bares its large canine teeth. However, on average only 20 per cent of a brown bear's diet is made up of animal flesh. Instead, bears rely on their large molars to crush their vegetable food.

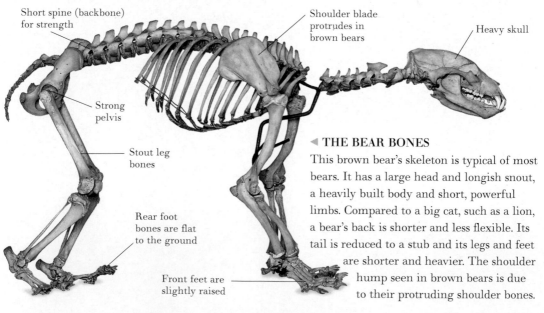

Short spine (backbone) for strength

Shoulder blade protrudes in brown bears

Heavy skull

Strong pelvis

Stout leg bones

Rear foot bones are flat to the ground

Front feet are slightly raised

◀ **THE BEAR BONES**
This brown bear's skeleton is typical of most bears. It has a large head and longish snout, a heavily built body and short, powerful limbs. Compared to a big cat, such as a lion, a bear's back is shorter and less flexible. Its tail is reduced to a stub and its legs and feet are shorter and heavier. The shoulder hump seen in brown bears is due to their protruding shoulder bones.

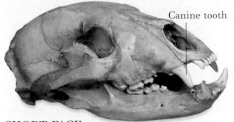

Canine tooth

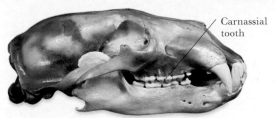

Carnassial tooth

▲ SHORT FACE

This brown bear's skull is shorter and more robust than that of the polar bear. North American brown bears tend to have larger skulls than bears in other parts of the world.

▲ LONG FACE

This polar bear's skull is longer and more slender than that of other bears. Like other carnivores, it has prominent, dagger-like canine teeth and meat-slicing carnassials at the back.

▲ PRIMITIVE BEAR

The spectacled bear is grouped separately from other bears. Apart from the giant panda, it is the most primitive bear. Its short muzzle and the unique arrangement of teeth in its jaw give it a more rounded head shape than its fellow bears.

▲ GIANT PANDA

The giant panda has the most massive skull in relation to its size of all living bears. Its round face and head are the result of large jaw muscles needed to grind tough bamboo stems.

▶ SLENDER SWIMMING BEAR

The polar bear has a more elongated body than other bears. Its neck and skull are relatively long and slim. These are adaptations that help the bear to swim through the water by streamlining its body. It also has lower shoulders, well-developed hindquarters and large, broad feet.

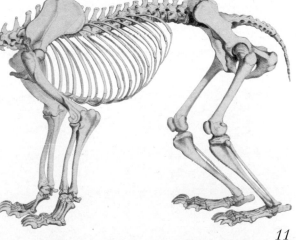

11

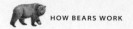

Strong Muscles

Bears are the bully-boys of the animal kingdom. Their strength is mainly in the muscles of their legs and shoulders. Unlike cats and dogs, which run on their toes for speed, bears walk on the flat soles of their broad feet, just as humans do. What bears lack in speed they make up for in strength. Their powerful, mobile limbs can be put to good use digging, climbing, fishing and fighting. They will attack others of their own kind and defend themselves ably from enemies. In a fight, a bear can do considerable damage and survives by sheer brute force. Male bears are generally much larger than females of the same species.

▲ CLAWS DOWN

The sun bear has particularly large, curved claws for climbing trees. It spends most of the day sleeping or sunbathing in the branches. At night it strips off bark with its claws, looking for insects and honey in bees' nests.

◀ PUTTING ON WEIGHT

This grizzly bear is at peak size. Most bears change size as the seasons pass. They are large and well-fed in autumn, ready for their winter hibernation. When they emerge in spring, they are scrawny with sagging coats.

BEOWULF

An Anglo-Saxon poem tells of the hero Beowulf (bear-wolf). He had the strength of a bear and went through many heroic adventures. Beowulf is famous for slaying a monster called Grendel. Here, Beowulf as an old man lies dying from the wounds inflicted by a fire-breathing dragon.

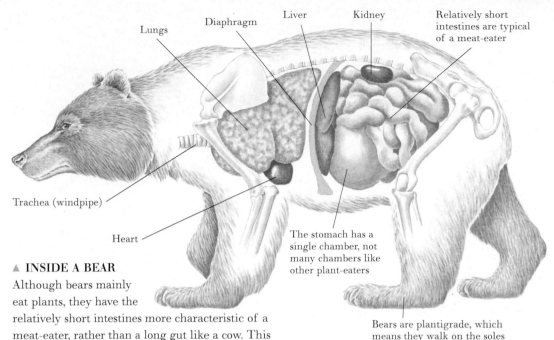

Lungs

Diaphragm

Liver

Kidney

Relatively short intestines are typical of a meat-eater

Trachea (windpipe)

Heart

The stomach has a single chamber, not many chambers like other plant-eaters

▲ INSIDE A BEAR

Although bears mainly eat plants, they have the relatively short intestines more characteristic of a meat-eater, rather than a long gut like a cow. This makes it hard for them to digest their food. Curiously, the bamboo-eating giant panda has the shortest gut of all. Because of this it can digest no more than 20 per cent of what it eats, compared to 60 per cent in a cow.

Bears are plantigrade, which means they walk on the soles of their feet

▲ SHORT BURSTS

Bears are not particularly agile and swift, but they can run fast over short distances. The brown bear can charge at 50km/h (lions reach about 65km/h) and does sometimes chase its food. A bear at full charge is a frightening sight and quickly scares away enemies.

▲ SWEET TOOTH

The sun bear's long slender tongue is ideal for licking honey from bees' nests and for scooping up termites and other insects. Like all bears it has mobile lips, a flexible snout and strong jaws.

13

Warm Fur

All bears have thick fur all over their bodies, including the face. Ground-living bears even have fur between the pads of their feet, while the soles of tree-climbing bears are naked. A thick coat insulates well in the cold, but can cause overheating in summer, so many bears moult. Most bears' coats tend to be brown, black, cinnamon (reddish-brown), grey or white and some have face and chest markings. The most strikingly marked bear is the giant panda. Its startling black and white pattern blends in with the shadowy bamboo of its mountain home. This is particularly so at dawn and dusk, the panda's most active times. In winter, against snow, black rocks and trees, the panda is almost invisible.

▲ **WHITE BEAR**
The Chinese call the giant panda *bei-shung* (white bear). It is considered to be basically white with black ears, eye patches, legs and shoulders. Sometimes the black areas have a chestnut reddish tinge.

▲ **VELVET COAT**
The sun bear has relatively short fur, a bit like velvet. It is generally black with a grey to orange muzzle and pale feet. Some bears have white or pale orange-yellow, crescent-shaped markings on the chest.

BERSERKIR
Among the most feared of Viking warriors were berserkirs. They were named after the bear pelts or bear-skin shirts they wore. Berserkirs worked themselves up into a frenzy before battle. We still use the Norse word berserk to mean crazy or wild. This walrus ivory berserkir is part of a chess set from the island of Lewis off the west coast of Scotland. The berserkir is shown biting his shield and clasping his sword in the rage of battle.

▲ BEAR FOOT

The broad, flat paw of a brown bear has thick fur on the upper surface and some between the toes, too. Ground-living bears, such as the brown bear, use their claws to hold on to a salmon or to catch and kill a young deer.

▼ SILVER TIP

The grizzly (American brown bear) gets its name from the way in which the long hairs of the shoulders and back are frosted with white. This gives the bear's coat a grizzled appearance. Brown bears, like the grizzly, are usually a dark brown colour, but they may also be any shade between light cream and black.

▲ FACIAL MARKINGS

The spectacled bear is generally dark brown or black. It has an unmistakable, spectacle-like pattern of white or yellowish hairs around the eyes and across the nose. These markings may extend to the chest.

► LONG HAIR

The sloth bear has long, black shaggy fur. The longest hair is between the shoulders. The black fur can be tinged with brown or grey. There is a white, or yellow to chestnut-brown, patch in the shape of a U or Y on the bear's chest. Chest markings may act as a warning sign when the bear stands up.

15

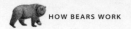

Life on the Ice

The polar bear is perfectly adapted to life in the frozen Arctic, where winter temperatures can drop to -50°C. Beneath its skin lies a thick layer of fat. The bear's entire body, including the soles of the feet, is covered in insulating fur made up of thick hairs with a woolly underfur. Each hair is not actually white, but translucent and hollow. This acts like a tiny greenhouse, allowing light and heat from the sun to pass through, trapping the warm air. Sometimes, such as in zoos, the hairs are invaded by tiny algae and the polar bear's coat has a green tinge. In the wild, the fur often appears yellow, the result of oil stains from its seal prey. Beneath the fur the skin is black, which absorbs heat. This excellent insulation keeps the polar bear's body at a constant 37°C.

RESPECT FOR THE ICE BEAR

The polar bear is the most powerful spirit in Arctic cultures. The Inuit believe that a polar bear has a soul. It will only allow itself to be killed if the hunter treats it properly after death. It is forbidden to hunt another bear too soon. Time must be left for the bear's soul to return to its family. Some Inuit offer a dead male bear a miniature bow and arrow, and a female bear a needle holder.

◀ **SEA-GOING BEAR**

Polar bears are excellent swimmers. They must swim frequently for their icy world is unpredictable. In winter, the Arctic Ocean freezes over. But with the arrival of storms and warmer weather the ice breaks up. Then the bear must swim between ice floes in search of seals. The thick layer of fat below the skin and dense, insulating fur allow a polar bear to swim in the coldest seas without suffering. In such cold water, a human being would be dead in a few minutes.

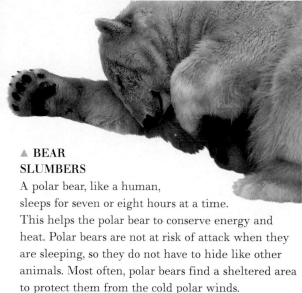

▲ COOLING DOWN

Polar bears are so well insulated they are in danger of overheating on warm days. To keep cool, they lie flat out on the ice. At other times they lie on their backs with their feet in the air.

▲ BEAR SLUMBERS

A polar bear, like a human, sleeps for seven or eight hours at a time. This helps the polar bear to conserve energy and heat. Polar bears are not at risk of attack when they are sleeping, so they do not have to hide like other animals. Most often, polar bears find a sheltered area to protect them from the cold polar winds.

▲ WARM BEARS

The insulating fur and fat of a polar bear is so efficient that little heat is lost. In fact, if a scientist were to look at a polar bear with an infra-red camera (which detects heat given off by the body), only the bear's nose and eyes would be visible.

▶ LAZY DAYS

Polar bears are most active at the start of the day. During summer, when the ice melts and retreats, bears may be prevented from hunting seals. Then they rest, living off their fat reserves and eating berries.

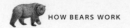

Using Brain and Senses

All bears are very intelligent. Size for size, they have larger brains than other carnivores, such as dogs and cats. They can remember sources of food and are very curious. Bears use their brains to find food or a mate, and to stay out of trouble. They are mainly solitary plant-eaters, however, so they have little need to think up hunting tactics or ways of communication. They rely on smell (the part of their brains that detects scent is the largest of any carnivore), with small eyes and ears compared to their head size. Bears often appear short-sighted, although they have colour vision to recognize edible fruits and nuts. People can easily chance upon a bear and take it by surprise, prompting the startled animal to attack in self-defence.

▼ SCENT MARKING
An American black bear cub practises marking a tree by scratching. When it is older, the bear will leave a scent mark to indicate to other bears that the territory is occupied.

◄ TEMPER TANTRUM
A threatened bear puts on a fierce display. First it beats the ground or vegetation with its front feet. Then it stands up on its back legs to look larger. This is accompanied by a high-pitched snorting through open lips or a series of hoarse barks. The display of aggression finishes with snapping the jaws together.

▲ FOLLOW YOUR NOSE

A brown bear relies more on smell than sight. It often raises its head and sniffs the air to check out who or what is about. It can detect the faintest trace of a smell, searching for others of its kind.

▼ GETTING TO KNOW YOU

Polar bear cubs rub against their mother to spread her scent over themselves. Smell allows a mother and cubs to recognize each other. They also communicate with sounds. Distressed cubs make low-pitched snores that develop into high whines.

BRUNO THE BEAR

Aesop's Fables are a set of tales written by the ancient Greek writer Aesop. One fable features Bruno the bear. He is shown as stupid and easily deceived. Bears were considered slow-witted because they sleep a lot. But Bruno was kind, unlike the cunning Reynard the fox. Bruno cared about others and forgave those who played pranks on him. Bruno was the forerunner of characters such as Winnie-the-Pooh.

▲ SNOWY SCENT TRAIL

Even in the Arctic, polar bears can pick up the trails of other bears and follow them. There are few objects around to use as scent posts for polar bears, so trails may be marked by the dribbling of urine on the ground.

Finding Food

Most bears eat whatever is available at different times of the year. They have binges and put on fat in times of plenty, then fast when food is scarce. Brown bears are typical of most bears in that they eat an enormous variety of food, from grasses, herbs and berries to ants and other insects. They also catch salmon and rodents, and on rare occasions hunt down bigger game, such as caribou, seals and birds. Only polar bears eat almost entirely meat, especially young seals. In summer, however, as the ice melts and they are unable to hunt, polars supplement their diet with grasses and berries. All bears, even the bamboo-loving panda, also scavenge on the carcasses of prey left by other animals. They are attracted to easy food, and rummage through rubbish thrown out into dustbins and left behind in campsites.

▶ **HUNTING DOWN A MEAL**

This American black bear has caught a white-tailed deer fawn. Both black and brown bears are successful hunters. They are able to ambush large animals and kill them by using their considerable bulk, strong paws and jaws. The size of the bear determines the size of its prey. Large brown bears may prey on moose, caribou, bison, musk ox, seals and stranded whales. Black bears are smaller than brown bears and take smaller prey, such as deer fawns, lemmings and hares. Roots, fruit, seeds and nuts, however, form up to 80 per cent of brown and black bears' diets.

GOLDILOCKS
The famous story of Goldilocks and the Three Bears *was first told in 1837. In the story, the bears and their ability to organize themselves properly are used to make a strong moral point. In contrast, Goldilocks is shown as a foolish, unthinking girl, who gets a nasty fright.*

▶ WALRUS CITY

Polar bears arrive on the northern coast of Russia each year to hunt walruses that have come there to breed. Enormous adult walruses shrug off attacks, but the young walrus pups are more vulnerable.

▲ BEACHCOMBING

Brown bears are attracted to beaches beside rivers and in estuaries. They overturn stones to feed on aquatic creatures, such as crabs and crayfish, that are hiding underneath.

▲ FRUIT LOVERS

An American black bear snacks on the ripe berries of a mountain ash tree. It carefully uses its incisors (front teeth) to strip the berries from their woody stem.

▲ INSECT EATERS

Two sloth bear cubs learn to dig up termites. The sloth bear uses its sickle-shaped claws to break open ant hills, bees' nests and termite mounds. Because it feeds mainly on termites, it has an ingenious way of collecting its insect food. First it blows away the dust. Then it forms a suction tube with its mouth and tongue, through which it can vacuum up its food.

Focus on

The giant panda specializes in eating bamboo, which forms over 99 per cent of its diet. Bamboo is plentiful and easy to harvest. Pandas consume the sprouts, stems and leaves. Digesting bamboo, however, is hard work. This is because the giant panda has a simple stomach and a short gut more characteristic of a carnivore. Most herbivores, such as cows, have several stomachs and very long intestines with bacteria inside that break down the plant tissue. The panda does not, so it must feed on huge quantities of bamboo (up to 40 kg) every day in order to keep going. Much of the leaf and stem matter passes through undigested.

MEAT AND TWO VEG

Whilst pandas spend most of their time eating bamboo, they do sometimes supplement their diet with meat when they can get it. They catch rats and beetles in the bamboo stands, and have been known to scavenge at leopard kills. But they make clumsy hunters and easy prey is scarce. In contrast bamboo is very abundant.

EARLY RISER

The giant panda is most active in the early morning and late afternoon. It spends 16 or more hours a day feeding and sleeps for up to four hours at a time. Most of the water a panda needs comes from bamboo. If it is thirsty, it scoops out a hollow by a stream. When this is full, the panda drinks all it can.

Bamboo Bears

ESSENTIAL FOOD

Umbrella bamboo and arrow bamboo are the giant panda's favourite food. Pandas also eat 28 other species of bamboo. They favour the leaves over the stems because these are the most nutritious parts and are easiest to digest. Pandas also eat other plants such as juniper, vines, holly and wild parsnip.

FEEDING ALL YEAR

Since bamboo is green and nutritious throughout the year, even in winter, the panda has a continuous supply of food. Unlike other bears, whose food is scarce at certain times, the panda has no need to hibernate, even when snow is covering its mountain home. A thick fur coat protects it from the cold.

TABLE MANNERS

A panda usually feeds sitting upright on its haunches. This leaves its forelegs free to handle bamboo. It manipulates the long stems of bamboo using its extra thumb (actually a modified wrist bone) on its front paws. It strips away the woody outer covering with its teeth. Then it pushes the stem at right angles into the corner of its mouth. Here, the centre part is crushed by large back teeth and then swallowed.

23

Climbing Trees

Trees provide food for some bears and a place of safety for others. Sun bears, sloth bears and spectacled bears climb trees regularly in search of food, such as fruits, seeds and nuts, as well as birds' eggs. Black bears are also agile tree-climbers. Polar bears rarely encounter trees. Those that move into the forest during the summer months, however, rest in hollows dug among tree roots to avoid the heat. Brown bear cubs climb trees to escape danger, but adult brown bears are too heavy to be good climbers. A female sloth bear will carry her small cubs into a tree on her back, unless she is escaping from a leopard since they can also climb trees! Most bears also use trees to mark their territory. They scratch the bark and rub on scents to tell other bears they are there.

◄ TREE-TOP HOME
The sun bear seeks out termite and bees' nests, and will rip away bark to get at insects hidden underneath. Although the sun bear feeds mainly on insects it also eats ripe fruit and preys on small rodents, birds and lizards.

► BEAR DANGER
A mother American black bear sends her cubs up into a tree while she stands guard at its base. If the danger is from an adult brown bear, the female will flee and return later for her cubs when the grizzly has gone.

▲ BELOW THE BARK
An adult, cinnamon-coloured American black bear is able to climb into a tree with ease using its short but sturdy claws. It can also lift bark to lick out insects with a long tongue.

▲ UP A TREE

Giant pandas stay mainly on the ground, but they will climb trees occasionally. They do so to sun themselves or to rest. Female pandas sometimes head up a tree to escape males, while males climb trees to advertise their presence.

▼ SAFE HAVEN

Black bears are normally found in forested areas. They have favourite trees located along trails where bears and other animals regularly pass. The bear marks the tree base with its scent and climbs into the branches where it is safe from brown bears.

▲ HIGH SCHOOL

Black bear cubs stay close to their mother both on the ground and in a tree. They watch and learn from her how to climb and find food among the branches.

Short, sturdy claws on a black bear's feet make tree climbing easy

▼ TREE HOUSE

Spectacled bears pull branches together to make a feeding platform. From here the bears feed mainly on tough plants called bromeliads. They also eat fruits, nuts, and honey and may take mice, rabbits and insects.

Gone Fishing

Brown and black bears sometimes overcome their reluctance to be with other bears when there is plenty of food available. This happens regularly on the rivers of the northwest coast of North America. Here, thousands of salmon come in from the sea and head upriver to spawn. The bears fish alongside each other at sites such as rapids where the water is shallower and the salmon are swimming more slowly. An uneasy truce exists between the bears, although isolated fights do occur. The salmon runs take place at different times of the year, but the most important are those in the months leading up to winter. The bears catch the oil-rich salmon to obtain the extra fat they need for the long hibernation ahead.

▲ **STRIPPED TO THE BONE**
Having caught a fish, the bear holds it firmly in its forepaws. Then it strips away the skin and flesh from the bones.

◀ **SALMON LEAP**
Salmon sometimes jump right into a bear's mouth. The bear stands at the edge of a small waterfall. Here the salmon must leap clear of the water to continue their journey upriver. All the bear needs to do is open its mouth!

◀ COME INTO CONFLICT

Sometimes the uncertain truce between bears breaks down and they fight for the best fishing sites in the river. Young bears playfight, but older ones fight for real. An open mouth, showing the long canine teeth, is a warning to an opponent. If the intruder fails to back down it is attacked. Fights are often soon over, because the bears are quick to return to the abundant source of fish.

▲ FISHING LESSON

Bear cubs watch closely as their mother catches a salmon. The cubs learn by example and will eventually try it themselves. It will be a long time before they are as skilful as their mother.

▲ A SLOUTHE OF BEERYS

A group of bears is called a sloth, so brown bears on a salmon river are a sloth of grizzlies. The term "a slouthe of beerys" was used in the Middle Ages. It came from people's belief at the time that bears were slow and lazy.

Focus on

Because it lives in one of the harshest and most unpredictable places on Earth, the polar bear is constantly on the look out for food. There may be four or five days between meals. Their most common prey is the ringed seal, although harp, bearded and hooded seals, or young walruses, are also taken. In spring, a bear searches for seal nursery dens. It breaks through the roof of snow and ice to reach the seal pups inside by jumping down with its powerful forelegs. During the rest of the year, a bear searches for holes in the ice where seals come up to breathe. While its eyesight and hearing are similar to ours, a polar bear's sense of smell is far superior. It can smell a den or breathing hole from a kilometre away.

1 A polar bear uses stealth and surprise to catch its prey. The bear approaches its target slowly, moving silently across the ice and swimming between ice floes. Its broad paws act like paddles and propel it effectively through the water. Its hind legs trail in the water and steer like a ship's rudder. A polar bear can also swim underwater to reach its prey, erupting from the sea to surprise seals resting on the edge of the ice.

2 A polar bear will stand or lie motionless for hours beside a good place for hunting. This may be at a seal's breathing hole or den. In spring, cracks form in the ice where it begins to melt. At points along the ice, seals emerge to rest or bask in the sun. A bear sniffs out suitable hauling-out places and lies in wait. Often, the bear's patience is not rewarded, for only one in fifty attempts to catch prey are successful.

Seal Hunting

3 A harp seal pops up to breathe through a hole in the ice. Before surfacing it would have looked for signs of danger. A bear usually lies on its stomach with its chin close to the edge of the ice. This conceals it from sight until the seal surfaces.

4 When a seal surfaces the bear scoops it out with a paw or grasps it around the head with its teeth and flips it out on to the ice. A powerful bite to the head crushes the seal's skull or breaks its neck and kills it instantly. The bear eats the fat and internal organs, but not the meat unless it is very hungry. It eats quickly since the smell of the kill might attract other bears.

5 Arctic foxes often follow polar bears across the ice in order to take advantage of their leftovers. Polar bears feed mainly on the seal blubber (fat), leaving behind most of the meat and bones. An average bear needs to eat 2kg of seal fat a day to survive. They have huge stomachs, enabling them to eat much more. After the meal, a polar bear cleans its fur by swirling in the water or rolling in the snow.

Winter Shutdown

Black bears, brown bears and pregnant female polar bears hibernate. They do so because food is scarce, not because of the cold. Scientists argued for years whether bears truly hibernate or merely doze during the winter months. Now, according to recent research, the hibernation of bears is thought to be even more complete than that of small mammals. During hibernation, a brown bear's heart rate drops to about 35 beats per minute, half its normal rate. American black bears reduce their blood temperature by at least one degree. They do not eat or drink for up to four months. Bears survive only on the fat that they have stored during the summer. A bear might have lost up to 50 per cent of its body-weight by the end of the winter.

▲ FAT BEARS

Before the winter hibernation a bear can become quite obese. Fat reserves make up over half this black bear's body-weight. It needs this bulk to make sure that it has sufficient fat on its body to survive the winter fast. In the weeks leading up to hibernation, a bear must consume large quantities of energy-rich foods, such as salmon.

Did you know?
Some hibernating bears sleep for 5½ months non-stop.

◀ HOME COMFORTS

A brown bear pulls in grass and leaves to cushion its winter den. American black bears and brown bears sleep in small, specially dug dens. These are usually found on the sunny, south-facing slopes of mountains.

▲ SNOW HOUSE

Female polar bears leave the drifting floes in winter and head inland to excavate a nursery den. They dig deep down into the snow and ice, tunnelling about 5m into the ground. Here they will give birth to their cubs. In severe weather, a male polar bear rests by lying down and allowing itself to be covered by an insulating layer of snow.

▲ SCANDINAVIAN REFUGE

A hole dug by a brown bear serves as its winter den in this Swedish forest. Bears spend winter in much stranger places, such as under cabins occupied by people, under bridges or beside busy roads.

▲ READY FOR ACTION

If disturbed, a bear wakes easily from its winter sleep. Although it is dormant, a bear's body is ready for action. It is able to defend itself immediately against predators, such as a hungry wolf pack.

▲ WINTER NURSERY

In the early winter, one bear enters a den, but three might emerge in spring. Female polar bears, like most bears, give birth (usually to twins) while hidden away in their dens. The tiny cubs are born in the middle of winter, in December or January.

A Solitary Life

Bears do not like other bears. They prefer to be alone. When two bears meet there is sometimes a fight, but usually it is just a shouting match and display. Young bears have playfights, not serious contests but rehearsals for battles later in life. Bears will break off hostilities when food is plentiful. Brown bears tolerate each other at fishing rivers and polar bears scavenge together at whale carcasses and rubbish dumps. But bears have to be constantly wary of other bears. Cannibalism (eating members of the same species) is more common in bears than in any other mammals. Male bears will fight and kill cubs. Deadly fights between adult male bears may end in one killing the other and then feeding on the loser's body.

▲ CANNIBALISM
Adult American male black bears and male polar bears are cannibals. They eat mainly younger bears. However, this sort of behaviour is thought to be relatively rare.

◀ ICE DANCE
Like two ballet dancers, young male polar bears play at fighting. They use exaggerated lunges and swipes with their paws and jaws. They do not hurt each other, but they must learn to fight well. Later in life as fully grown adults they will compete with other males for females during the breeding season. Fights between well-matched individuals can be violent and often bloody.

THE JUNGLE BOOK
Rudyard Kipling's famous story The Jungle Book *was first published in 1894. A young boy named Mowgli is brought up by wolves. He is befriended by Baloo the bear and Bagheera the panther who teach him the law of the jungle. The tiger Shere Khan plots to kill the man-cub.*

▲ **TRAGEDY ON THE ICE**
A mother polar bear stands over her cub, which has been mauled by a male. Male polar bears usually kill cubs for food. The female attacks and tries to drive the male away. Males are much bigger than females, but a female with cubs is a fierce opponent.

▲ **FRIENDS AT THE FEAST**
Brown bears gather to catch salmon at a popular spot in Alaska. If they get too close to each other, the bears will contest their fishing rights. Usually the larger bears succeed in fishing the best sites.

▲ **FISHING BREAK**
Young brown bears take a break from learning to fish and practise fighting instead. They fight by pushing and shoving at each other, using their enormous bulk to overcome their opponent. They also try to bite each other around the head and neck.

Meeting a Mate

Brown and black bears mate in the summer between May and July. Males use their well-developed sense of smell to track down females in heat. Brown bears often group together near rich food sources in the mating season, so males have to fight each other for the right to mate. Courtship between male and female bears is very brief, but when the male finds the female is ready to mate, he tries to isolate her from other males. The female is pregnant for from six to nine months. The length varies, because, no matter the time of mating, all the cubs are born at roughly the same time in the new year. This is because female bears delay the development of the fertilized egg in their wombs until late summer.

▲ COURTING COUPLE
A male and female brown bear may stay together for over a week during courtship and mate several times. The act of mating stimulates the female to release an egg. The male keeps other male bears away to be sure he is the father of any offspring.

◀ LOOK!
Male giant pandas often climb trees to advertise to females they are willing to mate. They wail, yap and bark to attract attention. Their loud calls also attract other males. The most dominant male mates with the female first. Pandas mate in spring.

▲ COURTSHIP DEADLOCK
A male has to overcome the female's natural tendency to be wary of him. The two assess each other with some gentle sparring interrupted by brief stand-offs and a lot of sniffing.

▼ HEAVENLY SCENT

Bears rely on their keen sense of smell to find a partner. An Alaskan brown bear approaches a receptive female, checking her odour track on the ground. If she lets him approach he sniffs her head, body and rear for signs that she is ready to mate. This period of courtship can last for up to 15 days, before the female is finally ready.

▶ ARCTIC ENGAGEMENT

Polar bears mate from late March to late May. They tend to congregate where there are plenty of seals. There are usually more males willing to mate than females. Like brown bears, a successful male tries to keep his temporary partner away from other male bears. They mate many times over a period of a week or more.

◀ MATING TIME

If a female brown bear is receptive, the male places his paw on her back. He mounts and grasps her in a bear hug, and bites the back of her head and neck. Mating is brief, lasting for only a few seconds up to about three minutes. The pair may mate up to 16 times in one day, and this may be repeated over several days. This ensures the female becomes pregnant by that particular male.

35

Nursery Dens

Most bears give birth hidden away from the outside world in dens. American black and brown bear cubs are born in winter, in January and February, when their mother is closeted in her winter den. A den can be a cave, in a hollow tree, under a tree that has been pushed over by the wind, or in a self-made hollow. Usually, two to three cubs are born, naked and helpless. Newborn bear cubs are small for the size of their mother. This is because a female bear's gestation period is very short. The mother has also to rely only on her fat reserves to build up their tiny bodies. A mother bear is only able to feed her cubs if she has eaten enough food in the months before her winter hibernation.

▲ **BLIND AND HELPLESS**
Ten-day-old brown bear cubs nestle into their mother's fur for warmth. With their eyes and ears tightly closed shut, they are totally dependent on her. The cubs remain in the den until May or June when they are about four months old.

Did you know? Polar bear cubs are no bigger than guinea pigs when born.

◄ **TWINS**
A polar bear mother tends her two young. The family leaves its den between late February and April depending on where they live. The further north they are, the later in the year they emerge.

▲ TRIPLETS
This American black bear has given birth to three healthy cubs. Females may have up to four cubs at one time. About the size of a rat and naked at first, the cubs grow quickly. They will leave the den in April or May.

▲ PANDA BABY
At Wolong breeding station in Sichuan, China, a baby giant panda is put in a box to be weighed. Giant pandas give birth to one or two cubs in a cave or tree hollow. If twins are born the mother often only rears one, leaving the other to die.

◄ MOTHER'S MILK
Three-month-old polar bear cubs suckle on their mother's milk. The milk is rich in fats and the cubs suckle for up to a year. Polar bear cubs are born covered with fine hair.

► IN THE DEN
American black bears weigh less than 300g when they are born in late January or early February. Their small size and lack of fur makes them vulnerable to the cold. The mother cleans and dries the cubs, then cuddles them close. The den is lined with branches, leaves, herbs and grasses to make a warm blanket. The mother spends a lot of time grooming her cubs and keeps the den scrupulously clean by eating their droppings.

Focus on

From late October, a pregnant female polar bear digs a snow den. Usually it is on a slope facing south, some distance from the sea. This is where she will give birth to her cubs. The mother warms her den with heat from her body. A tunnel to the nursery chamber slopes upwards so that warm air rises and collects in the chamber, which can be 20°C warmer than outside. She gives birth during the harshest part of winter from late November to early January, when permanent night covers the Arctic. The cubs grow fast. Around March the mother drives two holes through the walls of the den and helps the cubs to emerge for the first time.

1 A bank of snow makes an ideal site for a polar bear's winter den. The pregnant female bear digs into the south side of the snowdrift. The prevailing northerly winds pile up snow on the other side.

2 This etching shows an artist's impression of the inside of a polar bear's snow hole. The female bear gave birth to her cubs about three months ago. The cubs are now strong enough to follow their mother towards the sea where she can hunt and feed.

3 The female polar bear emerges from her winter home for the first time in the middle of March. The den's southward-facing entrance and exit hole faces towards the Sun, which is low on the horizon in early spring. The mother and her cubs are warmed by the Sun's rays.

Snow Homes

4 Sitting upright in a snow hollow, a female polar bear nurses her cubs. She differs from other female bears in having four working nipples rather than six. Her cubs also stay with her longer than most bears. She protects them from male bears until they are three years old. During this time she will teach her cubs how to survive in the cold Arctic conditions and also how to hunt seals.

5 On first emerging, the family remains at the den site for a few days so that the cubs become used to the cold. They play outside in the snow during the short days, and shelter in the den at night and during storms.

6 The cubs' first journey outside can be a long one. They may have to walk up to 22km to reach the sea ice where they will see their first seal hunt. The mother takes great care to avoid adult male bears who might try to kill her cubs.

Raising Cubs

Bear cubs spend the first 18 months to three years with their mother. If something should happen to her, they may be adopted by another mother with cubs the same age. The cubs learn everything from their mother. They learn to recognize the best foods and where and when to find them. They must also learn how to escape danger and how to find a winter den or shelter in a storm. Without this schooling, the young bears would not survive. Mothers and cubs can communicate by calling, particularly if they become separated or if a mother wants her offspring to follow her. During their development, cubs must keep out of the way of large male bears who might attack them.

▲ SAFE IN THE BRANCHES
Black bear cubs instinctively know that they should head for the nearest tree when danger threatens. It is easier for a mother to defend a single tree than a scattered family.

▼ MILK BAR
A mother brown bear suckles her twins. Her milk is thick and rich in fats and proteins, but low in sugars. It has three times the energy content of human or cow milk. The cubs are small at birth and must put on weight and grow quickly.

◄ LEAVING THE FAMILY

Young bears on their own, such as this brown bear, often become thin and scrawny. Despite being taught by their mothers where and how to feed, they cannot always find food. At popular feeding sites, such as fishing points, they are chased off by larger bears. When the time comes for young bears to look after themselves, the mother either chases them away or is simply not there when they return to look for her.

► LONG APPRENTICESHIP

Polar bear cubs are cared for by their mother for much longer than other bear cubs. They need to master the many different hunting strategies used by their mother to catch seals. These are not something that the cubs know instinctively, but rather skills that they must learn.

Did you know? Giant panda cubs are the first to leave their mothers at 18 months old

◄ FAMILY TRAGEDY

This polar bear cub is the victim in a tragic tug-of-war. A male bear has attacked the cub and its mother is trying to save it. Female polar bears fight ferociously to protect their young, but are often unsuccessful against larger opposition. Attacks like this, starvation, the cold and diseases mean that about 70 per cent of polar bear cubs do not live to their first birthday.

41

Where in the World are Bears?

Bears are found in a variety of habitats including the Arctic tundra, mountain slopes, scrub desert, temperate and tropical forests and tropical grasslands. Each species of bear, however, has its own preferred environment. The polar bear, for example, inhabits the lands and sea ice bordering the Arctic Ocean. It favours the shoreline areas where the ice breaks up and cracks appear, as this is where seals congregate. Most other bears are less specialized and have the uncanny ability to turn up wherever food is abundant. However, many of the wilderness areas where bears live are under threat. Habitat loss, as more land is cultivated for farmland and forests all over the world are cut down, is a major threat to many bears.

▲ **IN THE BAMBOO FORESTS**
The giant panda is restricted to areas of abundant bamboo forest. It was once much more widespread across eastern Asia, but now survives in just three provinces of western China – Gansu, Shanxi and Sichuan.

▼ **MOUNTAIN BEAR**
The spectacled bear lives in South America. It lives high in the Andes Mountains of Peru, Ecuador, Venezuela and Colombia. It is found in forests, including rainforests, cloud forests, and dry forests, as well as steppe (grassland) and rocky outcrops.

▲ **BROWN BEAR**
The brown bear is the most widespread of all bears. It is found in Europe, the Middle East, across Russia and northern Asia to Japan. North American brown bears live in Alaska and the Canadian Rockies.

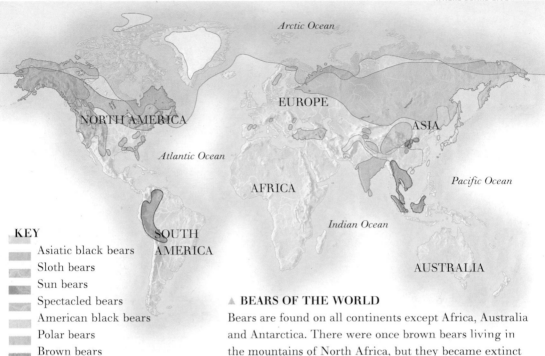

Arctic Ocean

NORTH AMERICA

EUROPE

ASIA

Atlantic Ocean

AFRICA

Pacific Ocean

SOUTH
AMERICA

Indian Ocean

AUSTRALIA

KEY

- Asiatic black bears
- Sloth bears
- Sun bears
- Spectacled bears
- American black bears
- Polar bears
- Brown bears
- Giant pandas

▲ BEARS OF THE WORLD

Bears are found on all continents except Africa, Australia and Antarctica. There were once brown bears living in the mountains of North Africa, but they became extinct (died out) in the 1800s.

▲ ASIATIC BLACK BEAR

The Asiatic black bear lives in mountainous regions over a wide area of southern and eastern Asia. It is found in northern India, Pakistan and on the islands of Japan and Taiwan.

▲ LIFE IN THE FOREST

The sloth bear (*above*) lives in dense, dry forests in India and Sri Lanka. The Malayan sun bear lives in similar lowland but tropical forests of South-east Asia. It is also thought to live in Yunnan in southern China, although no recent sightings have been reported.

Finding the Way

Bears have an uncanny knack of finding their way home even in unfamiliar territory. How they do this is only just beginning to be understood. For long distances, they rely on an ability to detect the Earth's magnetic field. This provides them with a magnetic map of their world and a compass to find their way around. When closer to home, they recognize familiar landmarks. In fact, bears have extraordinary memories, especially where food is involved. For example, a mother and her cubs are known to have trekked 32km to a favourite oak tree to feast on acorns. Five years later, the same cubs (now adults) were reported to have been seen at the same tree.

STARS IN THE SKY
The Great Bear constellation in the northern hemisphere is known to astronomers as Ursa Major. In Greek mythology, it was said to have been made in the shape of a she-bear and placed in the heavens by Zeus. The Great Bear is also worshipped in Hindu mythology as the power that keeps the heavens turning. The Inuit believe these stars represent a bear being continually chased by dogs.

▲ **ARCTIC NOMADS**
Polar bears are capable of swimming long distances between ice floes at speeds of up to 10km/h. They may travel thousands of kilometres across the frozen Arctic Ocean and the surrounding lands in search of prey.

▲ **BAD BEAR**
A sedated polar bear is transported a safe distance out of town. Nuisance bears are often moved this way but they unerringly find their way back.

GREENLAND

Baffin Island

North Western Territories

CANADA

Hudson Bay

Churchill

Quebec

Manitoba

Saskatchewan

Ontario

◄ **TO AND FROM THE FOREST**

The polar bears of Hudson Bay, Canada, migrate to the forests in summer and return to hunt on the sea ice in winter. On their return journey, they sometimes stop off at the town of Churchill. They gather at the rubbish dump to feed on leftovers, while they wait for ice to reform.

KEY

 Bears return to ice in winter

 Bears come ashore in June and July

 Bears walk north in autumn

▲ **REGULAR ROUTES**

Polar bears move quickly even on fast, shifting ice floes. A bear moving north, for example, against the southward-drifting ice in the Greenland Sea, can travel up to 80km in a day.

▲ **HAVING KNOWLEDGE**

Male brown bears live in large home ranges covering several hundred square kilometres. They must remember the locations of food and the different times of year it is available.

Focus on

Bears in some parts of the world are unique in terms of size or colour. Brown bears (grizzlies) on Kodiak, Shukak and Afongnak islands, Alaska, grow to a gigantic size. Across the Pacific, the brown bears of the Kamchatka Peninsula, Russia, are also giants. It is thought they reach their enormous size by including salmon as an important part of their diet.

Elsewhere, brown bears take the grizzly colour to an extreme and have fur resembling streaked hairstyles. American black bears show a very wide variation in colour. Many are not even black, ranging from white to red-brown. These variations may camouflage bears in different habitats. Black bears are invisible in dense forests, but lighter-coloured fur is an advantage in more open places.

BEAR GIANT
Standing on its hind legs, a Kodiak brown bear would tower over a person. It can weigh up to 750kg – almost as big as a North American bison. The average weight for a male Kodiak bear, however, is about 300kg. These bears are so powerful, they can kill and carry an adult moose.

CINNAMON BEAR
Cinnamon-coloured American black bears have a coat that is reddish brown to blond. Bears in the west tend to be cinnamon or honey-coloured, whereas bears in the east are mainly black.

Super Bears

BLUE BEAR
Blue or glacier black bears are found in north-west Canada. They have a blue-grey tinge to their fur. Like all American black bears, no matter what their body colour is, they have a brown muzzle.

RUSSIAN BEAR
The giant brown bears of the Kamchatka Peninsula, eastern Russia, have a varied diet. They eat the seeds of conifer trees, fish for salmon, hunt for seals and birds, and scavenge on stranded whales.

GHOST BEAR
One in ten black bears on Kermodes Island off North America's Pacific coast is snowy white. These bears are not albinos (animals that lack skin colour) or polar bears, but true black bears.

Ancient Bears

There were bears living in the past that were far bigger than today's huge Kodiak and polar bears. The giant short-faced bear, weighing over 1,000kg, was twice the size of a Kodiak. It is the largest known carnivorous (meat-eating) mammal to have ever lived on land. Bears, however, had much smaller beginnings. The first recognizable bear appeared about 20 million years ago. Called the dawn bear, it was about the size of a fox. Early bears split into three groups. The first group, the Ailuropodinae, followed a plant-based diet and of these only the giant panda still survives. The second group, Tremarctinae, included many species of short-faced bears whose only living relative today is the spectacled bear. The third group, Ursinae, includes most of the bears we see today as well as the now extinct cave bears.

Cave bear

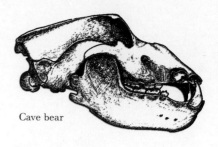

Brown bear

▲ BIG HEAD

The ancient cave bear (*Ursus spelaeus*) had a bigger skull than modern brown bears. Its high-domed skull anchored powerful chewing muscles. Enormous back teeth show that it mainly ate plants. It died out about 10,000 years ago.

◄ DAWN BEAR

Evolving from an animal that looked part dog, part bear and part raccoon, the dawn bear (*Ursavus elmensis*) was the ancestor of all known bears living today. Twenty million years ago it probably spent most of its time hunting in the tree-tops. By studying its teeth, scientists think the dawn bear supplemented its diet of meat with plant material and insects.

▶ **GIANT SHORT-FACED BEAR**

The giant short-faced bear
(*Arctodus simus*) had much
longer legs than today's bears and
probably ran down its prey. In profile it
resembled a big cat. In its jaws were canine teeth
capable of delivering a killing bite and back teeth
for shearing meat. It probably hunted ancient
camels, bison and horses that once lived on the
plains of North America. The only living
descendant of the short-faced bear is the
spectacled bear (*Tremarctos ornatus*), the sole
species of bear to be found in South America.

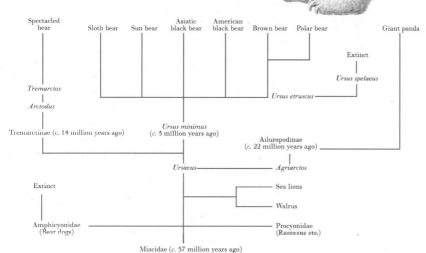

◀ **FAMILY OF BEARS**

This chart shows
how ancient bears
gave rise to modern
ones. The more
ancient bears are at
the bottom and
modern bears are at
the top.

◀ **GREAT EUROPEAN CAVE BEAR**

About 500,000 years ago, the cave
bear (*Ursus spelaeus*) evolved.
It was about the size of today's
Kodiak bears, with massive front legs,
broad paws with claws, and a huge
head and large muzzle. Large quantities
of bones found in caves throughout
Europe indicate that many died during
winter hibernation, probably because they
failed to put on enough fat to survive until spring.

Family Groups

The eight species of living bears belong to the family Ursidae. They all have the same general appearance, but in different parts of the world, each is adapted to a particular lifestyle. Bears in tropical places tend to be small and spend more time in the trees. Those in northern lands are larger and live mostly on the ground. To help them study bears, scientists divide the eight living species into three smaller groups, or subfamilies. The giant panda and spectacled bear are the sole survivors of two ancient subfamilies, the Ailuropodinae and Tremarctinae. The rest of the bears are grouped together in a third subfamily, the Ursinae. A bear's Latin name reveals how that particular species is grouped.

▲ SLOTH BEAR

Very little is known about the origins of the Indian sloth bear (*Melursus ursinus*). Few fossils (remains preserved in stone) have been found for this species of tropical bear. Sloth bears are thought to have evolved during an ice age that started about 1.6 million years ago.

◀ BROWN BEAR

Brown bears (*Ursus arctos*) first appeared in China about 500,000 years ago. From here they migrated right across the northern hemisphere into North America and Europe.

▲ POLAR BEAR

The polar bear (*Ursus maritimus*) is the most recent bear to have evolved. Its closest relative is the brown bear. In zoos, polar bears and brown bears are sometimes interbred.

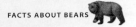

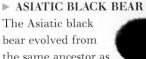 **ASIATIC BLACK BEAR**

The Asiatic black bear evolved from the same ancestor as most other species of bear, *Ursus minimus*. It is found mainly in the hilly areas of southern Russia, Japan, and southern Asia. This bear is in danger of extinction in some areas, because it is still hunted for food and medicine.

▲ **GIANT PANDA**

The giant panda (*Ailuropoda melanoleuca*) is the sole survivor of the earliest group of bears, the Ailuropodinae. It first appeared around 10 million years ago. Fossils of giant pandas have been found throughout China.

 ▼ **SUN BEAR**

The sun bear (*Helarctos malayanus*) is another tropical bear about which very little is known. It too probably evolved during the last Ice Age. Today sun bears are under threat from pressures such as farming. The bears tear out the hearts of oil palms, which ruins the crop.

▼ **SPECTACLED BEAR**

The spectacled bear (*Tremarctos ornatus*) evolved about 2 million years ago. It is the last remaining member of a group of primitive short-faced bears (Tremarctinae) that were found mainly in the Americas.

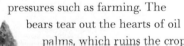

Relatives and Impostors

Bears are included in the order Carnivora, a group of mammals that includes cats, dogs and hyenas. The bears' nearest relatives are the raccoon, dog and weasel families. Bears are also probably the closest living relatives of seals and sea lions, members of the order Pinnipedia. The skull of the polar bear, for example, is very similar to that of a seal. Most relatives of bears are meat-eaters, unlike many bears themselves. Some, such as weasels, are loners, much like bears, while others, such as wolves, live in groups and hunt together. A few animals have a strong similarity to bears, but are in fact not related at all. The wombat and koala, two types of marsupial (mammals that raise their young in a pouch), are often confused with bears but are totally unrelated.

▲ **KOALA**
The Australian koala is very similar in appearance to a small bear. It is commonly called the koala bear, but it is not a bear at all. It is a more primitive mammal and is a member of the order Marsupiala. Members of this order, marsupials, have pouches in which their young develop.

◄ **RACCOON**
Raccoons have been given the name washing bear. This may be because of the way they use their front paws to locate prey. They look like they are washing their prey before eating it. Raccoons are not bears, but they are related to them.

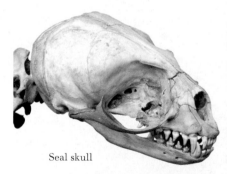

Seal skull

▲ **ARCTIC SIMILARITIES**
Seals and bears are distant relatives. Polar bear and seal skulls have long muzzles, parallel rows of teeth and flattened bones protecting the ear.

▲ THE LONG-TAILED KINKAJOU

The kinkajou is known as the honey bear, but it is not a real bear. It is a South American member of the raccoon family. It spends most of its life in the trees feeding mainly on fruit. It is also very fond of honey. A prehensile (grasping) tail helps it grip on to branches.

▲ DISTANT RELATIVES

Hyenas, unlike bears, live in groups in which the females are the leaders. They have a reputation as scavengers, but are also effective predators. By hunting together they can bring down large prey. Hyenas share a common early ancestor with bears, but are actually more closely related to cats.

▲NO RESEMBLANCE

The weasel is a solitary carnivore, like the bear. Stoats and weasels share the same ancestor as bears, raccoons and dogs. However, over millions of years, all of these animals have evolved very different characteristics and body shapes.

▶ HUNGRY LIKE A WOLF

The grey wolf is a member of the dog family. It often lives in the same places as brown and black bears. It hunts in packs and sometimes targets the same prey as bears, such as moose and caribou.

Pandas on the Edge

Pandas are the rarest of all bears. Each year their habitat shrinks. There are just 25 pockets of panda forest remaining, each with no more than 50 wild pandas living there. This makes pandas extremely vulnerable. One threat is the flowering of bamboo. When bamboo flowers it dies back. Each species of bamboo flowers at a different time. In the past, pandas would leave their home range and travel to where other species of bamboo were not flowering. Today, pandas are trapped by the surrounding farmland and cannot move from one bamboo stand to another. The Chinese government is desperately trying to conserve the panda. Reserves have been set up to study panda behaviour and establish breeding programmes. The panda is regarded as a national treasure. Anyone killing a panda faces the death penalty.

▲ FEEDING TIME
A baby giant panda is bottle-fed at a panda breeding centre in China. By giving the babies a helping hand early in life, it is hoped more pandas may grow to adulthood. They may then be returned to their native bamboo forests.

Did you know? Baby pandas are blind, pink and weigh just 100g at birth.

◀ CAPTIVE BREEDING
These are two of the 100 or so giant pandas in zoos and breeding centres worldwide. Unfortunately pandas are slow to have young. Artificial insemination is used in attempts to breed more pandas in captivity.

▲ SYMBOL FOR CONSERVATION

The World Wide Fund for Nature adopted the giant panda as its logo. Its rarity and universally popular appeal has made the panda a natural ambassador for all living things facing extinction.

▲ ON DISPLAY

This giant panda is far from its natural home. The chances are that it has not been bred in a zoo but taken from the wild. It is, however, safe from poachers who supply a lucrative market in panda skins.

◄ PANDA TRANSPORT

Chinese biologists in the Wolong Reserve, Sichuan, try to persuade a giant panda to enter a cage. They will move the panda to the breeding centre for further studies. It is only since the 1980s that scientists have started to understand the panda's biology.

► BACK TO THE WILD

Many pandas have been born in captivity, but less than a third of cubs have survived. It was hoped that captive-bred pandas could be returned to the wild, but the results are disappointing. This is because there is not enough vacant habitat to return captive pandas to. There are now 13 panda reserves and these cover about half the remaining habitat.

Focus on

Polar bears come into close contact with people each autumn at the isolated Canadian town of Churchill on the shores of Hudson Bay. The bears are on their way from the forests inland where they spend the summer, to the ice of the bay where they hunt. Often they arrive before the ice forms and cause a lot of trouble while they hang around with nothing to do. Some bears head for town and scare the local townsfolk. Others head for the town dump. The bears are chased away, but frequent offenders are tranquillized and transported somewhere safe. The bears, however, have become a tourist attraction. People come from all over the world to see the congregations of polar bears, which are usually much more solitary in the wild.

LOOKING FOR TROUBLE
This bear has picked up the tantalizing scent of tourists. Many visitors arrive to see the bears each year. They travel about in great buses called tundra buggies, where they are safe from the powerful and inquisitive bears.

OVERSTEPPED THE MARK
A researcher cautiously tests a tranquillized polar bear to make sure it is fully sedated. He holds a gun in case the polar bear is not as sleepy as it seems and attacks. Polar bears at Churchill occasionally threaten people. They are tranquillized and moved a safe distance away or locked up in a trap until the ice refreezes.

Churchill

BEAR BACK

A polar bear keeps cool by rolling in a patch of snow while it waits for the ice to form on Hudson Bay. The days can be warm in the Arctic autumn. Polar bears have thick fur and may overheat if they are not able to cool down.

FAST FOOD

A bear scavenges through the town rubbish dump. This is a favourite rendezvous spot. Household rubbish provides easy food for hungry bears unable to hunt.

FREE FLIGHT

A sedated bear is carried away in a net strung under a helicopter. This is a quick way to move a large animal, but it is also very expensive.

THE SIN BIN

A rogue bear is released from a bear trap. Unfortunately, bears have a well-developed homing instinct and often appear in town again. Persistent offenders are kept in a polar bear jail until the ice refreezes.

DANGER
BEAR TRAP

▲ GREAT ESCAPE
A hiker takes refuge in a tree after surprising a brown bear on a trail in Montana, USA. Adult brown bears do not climb trees. The hiker will have to wait for the bear to lose interest before he can come down.

Bears and People

Bears can be dangerous. They are attracted to food at campsites and rubbish dumps and here they come into contact with people. Fatal attacks by bears are rare. A person walking in bear country is seldom attacked, as long as the bear knows that they are there. Walkers are advised to make a lot of noise, clapping their hands and singing, for example, to warn any bears in the vicinity of their presence. Black bears tolerate people more readily than brown bears or grizzlies. Brown bears, because they have poor eyesight, might mistake people for a threat and charge. Whatever happens, a walker should never come between a mother bear and her cubs, as she will certainly fiercely defend them.

◄ BEGGING FOR FOOD
People driving in national parks in the USA offer titbits to black bears, despite warnings not to. The animals have learnt to associate cars with food. To get inside a car bears have been known to break windows or use their claws like a can-opener to slice through metal doors.

▲ BEAR WARNING

Signs warn visitors to behave sensibly. Even so, a bear might attack. It acts aggressively at first, chomping its jaws together and hitting the ground. It then charges but usually stops at the last moment.

▲ TRAPPED IN THE ZOO

A bear gnaws the bars of its tiny cage in a zoo in Tunisia. Bears are very popular animals, but they are often kept in terrible conditions in small zoos. This concrete-lined cage is totally bare and does not provide an interesting and stimulating home.

Did you know? Since 1900, there have been fewer than 150 attacks on people in the US.

▲ LOOKING FOR FOOD

The tempting smells coming from a dustbin are irresistible to a hungry bear. Unfortunately, bears begin to associate people with easy food. Harmless scavenging can become dangerous if the bear fails to get the food that it wants.

▲ DANGEROUS SITUATION

Bears and people cross paths occasionally. These people are too close to a brown bear for their own safety. If possible, bears should be given a wide berth. They will usually ignore or avoid people, and can be watched safely from a distance.

Bears in Danger

Of the eight species of bears living today, six are considered to be endangered. Only polar bears and American black bears are holding their own, and even they would not survive without considerable protection. Bears face many dangers. Their habitat is shrinking as natural areas are used to provide homes and farmland for people. Cubs are kept as pets but sold when they grow into troublesome adults. Many wild bears do not reach old age because they are shot by hunters. Hides and heads are used as wall hangings and trophies. In many parts of the world bear meat is eaten as a delicacy. Blood, bones and body parts are used in traditional Oriental medicines and as good luck charms. By far the biggest threat to bears is from poaching to supply the medicine trade.

▲ DANCING BEAR
A sloth bear is made to dance in India. Despite laws against it, bear cubs are taken from the wild. They are taught to dance using cruel methods and kept in poor conditions.

◀ BEAR CIRCUS
Bears have long been a popular act in circuses. Their ability to walk on their hind feet makes them appear almost human. These agile and clever animals are forced to perform tricks such as skipping, riding a bicycle and walking the tightrope. Performing bears are sometimes badly cared for and may be made to work all year round.

▲ ANCIENT PERSECUTION

Bears have been entertaining people for centuries. This carving from the AD300s depicts gladiators fighting bears in the arena. Both brown bears and polar bears were killed to entertain the audience.

◄ HEALING

We can learn a lot from bears. Native Americans discovered that many plants eaten by bears have medicinal properties. The Cheyenne treat diarrhoea with a plant called bear's food and the Crow use bear root to cure sore throats.

Spinal cord treats deafness

Bones cure rheumatism

Gall bladder purifies the blood, lowers temperature and reduces inflammation

Blood cures nervousness in children

Paws prevent colds

▲ MEDICINE CHEST

Bear organs are important in Oriental medicine. The most valuable part is the gall bladder, said to cure a whole host of ailments including fevers. Many bears are killed for their gall bladder alone.

► MEASURING UP

A scientist takes measurements from a tranquillized bear. A better understanding of the biology and behaviour of bears will hopefully secure them a safer future.

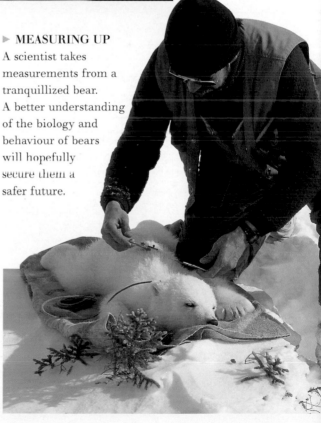

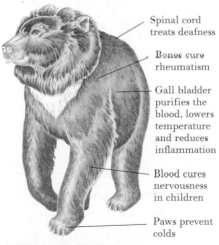

61

GLOSSARY

adaptation
A change in a living thing to suit a new set of conditions. This change helps the animal (or plant) to survive in its environment.

algae
A group of very simple plants, some of which are only the size of a single cell. Others are much larger. Most types of algae live in water, but they also grow on damp soil and tree trunks.

bacteria
A type of microorganism – a living thing that cannot be seen by the naked eye. Huge numbers of bacteria live in the soil and break down dead material. Millions of bacteria live in the gut and on the skin of many animals, including humans.

canine
A sharp, pointed tooth used for killing and holding prey.

carnassial
A strong, shearing tooth at the back of a carnivore's mouth.

carnivore
An animal that feeds partly or mainly on the flesh of other animals.

conservation
Protecting living things and helping them to survive in the future.

continent
One of the seven main land masses on Earth. The continents are North America, South America, Europe, Africa, Asia, Australia and Antarctica.

cultivation
The preparation and use of the ground in order to grow crops.

diet
The usual types of food eaten by an animal.

digestion
The process by which food is broken down so that it can be taken into the body.

dormant
When an animal lies motionless and inactive, as in sleep.

environment
The surroundings in which an animal or plant lives. It includes both living things (other animals and plants) and non-living things (such as stones, the air, temperature and sunlight).

estuary
The tidal mouth of a large river, where it flows into the sea.

evolution
The gradual development of new types of living things from existing species over very long periods of time.

extinction
When a whole species or larger group of animals or plants disappears, dying out completely.

fable
A story, often with a mystical theme, which is not based on fact.

fertilization
The joining together of a male sperm and a female egg to start a new life.

genetic
Relating to the genes, inside the cells. Genes control the characteristics passed on from parents to their offspring.

grizzly bear
Another name for the brown bear. It is particularly used to mean North American brown bears.

habitat
A place that has certain kinds of animals and plants living there, such as tropical rainforest or semi-desert.

herbivore
An animal that eats plants.

hibernation
A period of sleep during the winter when body processes slow down. Animals hibernate mainly because food is scarce and they might starve otherwise.

Ice Age
A time when large parts of the Earth were covered by glaciers and ice. The last Ice Age ended about 10,000 years ago.

ice floe
A sheet of ice floating in the sea.

incisor
Front tooth used for biting off chunks and cutting up meat.

insulation
A covering, such as a layer of thick fat beneath a polar bear's skin, that prevents heat leaving a warm body to the cold outside.

intestine
Part of an animal's gut where food is broken down and absorbed into the body.

Inuit
A people of the Arctic region, also known as Eskimos. The word Inuit, which means people, is preferred because Eskimo means eaters of raw meat and the Inuit cook at least part of their diet.

mammal
An animal with fur or hair and a backbone, which can control its own body temperature. Female mammals feed their young on milk made in mammary glands in their bodies.

mating
The pairing up of a male and female to produce young. During mating, the fertilization of an egg with a sperm takes place.

migration
A regular journey some animals make from one place to another, because of changes in the weather or their food supply, or to breed.

molar
A broad, ridged tooth in the back of a mammal's jaw, used for grinding up food.

nipple
A teat through which young suck milk from the mammary glands.

playfight
Early preparation for learning how to fight when cubs are older. Playing helps to build up muscles, improve co-ordination and develop good reflexes.

predator
An animal that catches and kills other animals (prey) for food.

prehensile tail
A tail that is capable of grasping and holding on to objects such as branches.

prey
An animal that is hunted for food by another animal (predator).

rainforest
Dense forest that is wet all year round.

scavenge
Feed on the remains of a kill left behind by another animal or on naturally dead animals or rubbish.

spawn
Produce eggs in large numbers to be fertilized.

species
A group of animals that share similar characteristics and can breed together to produce young.

streamline
The rounded, tapering shape that allows water (or air) to flow smoothly around an object.

subspecies
A species is sometimes divided into even smaller groups called subspecies, which are sufficiently distinct to have their own group.

suckle
Suck milk from the breast of a female mammal.

temperate
Mild regions of the Earth that do not experience extreme heat or cold, wet or dry.

territory
An area in which an animal or group of animals live. The borders of territories are marked, so that others of the same species know to keep out.

trail
A path through the forest or open ground that an animal such as a bear uses regularly.

tropical
Warm, wet regions of the Earth, near the Equator.

tundra
A treeless region of the Earth with permanently frozen soil just below the surface.

womb
An organ in the body of female mammals in which young grow and are nourished until birth.

INDEX

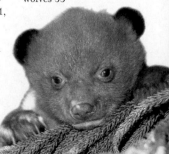